IN MEMORY OF

ELEANOR VAN HORNE

PRESENTED BY

FRIENDS AND FAMILY
1993

A Tribute to
THE YOUNG AT HEART

DR. SEUSS

By Jill C. Wheeler

Published by Abdo & Daughters, 6535 Cecilia Circle, Edina, Minnesota 55439.

Library bound edition distributed by Rockbottom Books, Pentagon Tower, P.O. Box 36036, Minneapolis, Minnesota 55435.

Printed in the United States.

Cover Photo: FPG
Inside Photos: Bettmann News Photo 4, 16, 20, 25 & 30
                 Archive Photos 8, 14 & 18
                 FPG 12, 27 & 32
                 UN Photo 21

Edited by Rosemary Wallner

LIBRARY OF CONGRESS CATALOGING-IN-PUBLICATION DATA

Wheeler, Jill C., 1964-
    Dr. Seuss / written by Jill C. Wheeler; [edited by Rosemary Wallner].
        p. cm. -- (The Young at Heart)
    Summary: Discusses the life and works of Thedor Geisel.
    ISBN 1-56239-112-7 (lib. bdg.)
    1. Seuss, Dr. -- Juvenile literature. 2. Authors, American -- 20th century -- Biography -- Juvenile literature. 3. Children's literature, American -- History and criticism -- Juvenile literature. [1. Seuss, Dr. 2. Authors, American. 3. Illustrators.] I. Wallner, Rosemary, 1964- . II. Title. III. Series: Wheeler, Jill C., 1964-   Young at Heart.
PS3513.E2Z96 1992   813'.52--dc20   92-16569
                                          [B]

International Standard Book Number:	Library of Congress Catalog Card Number:
1-56239-112-7	92-16569

TABLE OF CONTENTS

Theodore S. Geisel, "Dr. Seuss," with his infamous mischief maker, the Cat in the Hat.

4

HAVE YOU EVER SEEN A SNEECH?

Nearly every library in America has a Sneech on its shelves. The Sneeches are right beside the Yooks and the Once-lers and the Who's of Whoville. And they're beside the Cat in the Hat and Horton the elephant and Thidwick the moose.

Most people have seen a Sneech in the pages of a book. Some have seen Horton on TV. But long before these creatures inhabited bookshelves and TV screens, they haunted the imagination of a special man.

Theodor Geisel, more commonly known as Dr. Seuss, spent a lifetime dreaming up fantastical creatures with tongue-twisting names. Over the years, he has shared his vivid imagination through forty-six different storybooks. Publishers have translated his books into twenty different languages for the world to enjoy.

Many people were sad when Dr. Seuss died in 1991. Yet he left a part of himself behind for all to enjoy. His creatures made both children and adults laugh out loud.

They also told some important stories that will be read again and again and again.

ZOOS, SCHOOLS AND DOODLES

Theodor Geisel was born in Springfield, Massachusetts, on March 2, 1904. As a young boy he drew many pictures. Sometimes, his parents wondered if their son had too much of an imagination. He was always drawing strange-looking people and animals on his schoolbooks. He made up funny names for them. The drawings made him and his sister, Margaretta, laugh.

Geisel's father worked for a brewery until 1920 when the United States passed a law called Prohibition. Prohibition made it illegal for people to brew and drink alcohol. "My father was going to be made president of the brewery the day Prohibition was declared," Geisel recalled. "It made him sort of cynical."

Since he could no longer be a brewer, Geisel's father became a part-time zookeeper and parks superintendent. Geisel liked to go with him to the zoo. He drew the animals he saw there. He often thought about how he would run the zoo if it were his job.

Geisel continued to doodle and imagine stories as he grew up and went to school. After he graduated from high school in Springfield, he went to Dartmouth College in Hanover, New Hampshire. His goal was to be a professor. Yet even in college, he couldn't stop drawing. He drew cartoons for the college magazine.

After graduating in 1925, Geisel went to another school – Oxford University in England. He wanted to study for a doctorate in literature. While he was there, he met a young American woman named Helen Palmer. The two of them spent a lot of time together.

Geisel decided to leave Oxford and travel throughout Europe. But he did not want to leave Helen Palmer. He asked her to be his wife. They were married in 1927.

After graduating in 1925, Geisel went to Oxford University in England. He wanted to study for a doctorate in literature.

QUICK, HENRY! THE FLIT!

After his tour of Europe, Geisel began looking for a job in the United States. He earned money drawing cartoons for magazines. He also sold his drawings as artwork for advertisements and wrote copy for some ads.

One of his ad campaigns was called "Quick, Henry! The Flit!" His drawing in the ad showed a person being attacked by giant insects.

Geisel did well in advertising but he did not enjoy it. He wanted to do something else. But at the time, the U.S. was in the middle of the Depression. During the Depression, millions of people were out of work. They barely could get enough money to eat. Geisel knew he had to do whatever he could to feed himself and his wife. "I was successful but frustrated," he said of that time in his life.

Geisel worked in advertising for fifteen years, but he pursued other interests in his spare time. He began writing and illustrating an alphabet book for children. He was very excited about his book, and he showed it to many publishers. One after another, the publishers rejected the book.

Geisel was heartbroken. He didn't try to writing a children's book again for several years.

Then, in 1936, he decided to go back to Europe. He took a ship across the Atlantic and spent many hours at the railing listening to the sounds of the ship's engines. Slowly, the sounds made a musical tune in his head, and he began imagining a parade.

The parade began with a horse and a wagon. As the parade passed, it became more and more unbelievable. The final part of the parade had an airplane showering spectators with brightly colored confetti.

When he got a chance, Geisel wrote down what he had imagined while on the ship. It became a book called *And to Think That I Saw It on Mulberry Street.* Excitedly, Geisel showed it to forty-three different publishers. Every one of them rejected his book.

Finally in 1937, a friend published it for him. The book became very popular. Millions of children still read it today. The book also was the first time Geisel used his pen name of Dr. Seuss. Seuss had been his mother's last name before she married.

WRITING NOVELS AND MAKING MOVIES

Geisel was proud of his *Mulberry Street* book. Yet he had always dreamed of writing novels, too. In 1939, he published a book he had written for adults. It was called *The Seven Lady Godivas*. Unfortunately, few people liked his novel and the book failed.

Several years later, Geisel had an opportunity to do something completely new. The U.S. was at war, and Dr. Seuss became Army Captain Geisel. The Army sent him to Hollywood, California, to write scripts for informational films called documentaries. He also drew, or animated, cartoons.

Many people praised Geisel's work. After the war ended, he won an Academy Award for a film he had written and an Oscar for a cartoon he ani-mated. He also had offers from people who wanted him to write screenplays for them.

Geisel turned down the offers to write screenplays. "I found I preferred making my own mistakes rather than being told how to make them," he said. "So I went back to writing kids' books."

The U. S. was at war, and Dr. Seuss became Army Captain Geisel.

Geisel turned his back on writing screenplays, but he could not turn his back on California. In 1948, he and Helen moved to a new home near La Jolla, California. The house was built around an old watchtower on a hill overlooking the Pacific Ocean. Geisel turned the top of the tower into his office. There, he spent eight hours a day writing, dreaming and drawing.

BATTLING ILLITERACY

In the early 1950s, a man named John Hersey began studying how school children learned to read in a Connecticut school. He wrote a report telling what he had learned. In May 1954, the popular magazine *Life* published part of Hersey's report.

Hersey's report said children were having problems learning to read because their books were so boring. At that time, most children learned to read through stories about characters called Dick, Jane and their dog, Spot. The books used only a few simple words.

In the 1950's, John Hersey studied how school children learned to read.

Geisel's publisher saw the article in *Life*. He sent Geisel a list of 400 words that were important to beginning readers. He asked Geisel to cut the list down to 250 words. He believed first grade readers could absorb only that many words at one time.

Geisel viewed the assignment as a challenge. Still, he wasn't sure where to start. How did a person write a book with only 250 words? What would the story be?

"I almost threw the job up," Geisel said. "I finally gave it one more chance and said, 'If I find two words that rhyme and make sense to me, that's the title.' So I found cat rhymed with hat. And like a genius, I said, 'That's the name.'"

Nine months later, Geisel had written *The Cat in the Hat* using only 220 words. The book was an instant success. It was also Geisel's first effort in the fight against illiteracy. Illiteracy is when people cannot read enough to live comfortably.

After he published *The Cat in the Hat* in 1957, Geisel put in many hours encouraging people of all ages to learn to read. He and Helen started the Beginner Books division of Random House Publishing in 1958.

*Dr. Seuss stands by as workmen raise a giant
"Cat in the Hat" billboard to the roof of the San Diego Muesum of Art.*

The Beginner Books division publishes simple books which young people can read to themselves.

FIFTY BUCKS FOR FIFTY WORDS

Geisel loved a challenge. A challenge spurred him to write *The Cat in the Hat*. A few years later, his publisher, Bennett Cerf, gave him a new challenge. Cerf bet Geisel $50 that he couldn't write an entire book using only fifty words.

"I did it to show I could," Geisel said about why he accepted the bet. The result was a book called *Green Eggs and Ham*. The book, about a creature who tries to get his friend to eat green eggs and ham, uses only fifty different words. *Green Eggs and Ham* was published in 1960.

The book was a hit among young readers. It also was a hit with the author. Geisel once said *Green Eggs* was "the only book I ever wrote that still makes me laugh." He liked to remind people that Cerf had never paid him the $50.

*Bennett Cerf bet Geisel $50 that he couldn't
write an entire book using only fifty words.*

Not all of Geisel's books were inspired by challenges. Once, Geisel was sitting in his office with the windows open. A breeze lifted a piece of paper with an elephant sketched on it and laid it down on another drawing of a tree.

"All I had to do was figure out what that elephant was doing in that tree, and I had a book," Geisel recalled. He decided the elephant was sitting on a nest in a tree. The elephant, named Horton, was taking care of the egg for a lazy bird named Mayzie. The story became *Horton Hatches the Egg.*

Other Dr. Seuss stories came from Geisel's own interests. His book *If I Ran the Zoo* was based on his childhood fantasies. He wrote another Horton book, *Horton Hears a Who*, after he visited Hiroshima. Hiroshima is a city in Japan that was destroyed in World War II, killing many people. *Horton Hears a Who* is about the importance of every life.

The Butter Battle Book is about the nuclear arms race. It is a story about the Zooks and the Yooks. The Zooks eat their bread buttered-side down. The Yooks eat their bread buttered-side up.

Eventually, the two sides get into a fight because of the way they eat their bread. Geisel wanted the book to show people can silly they are when they fight.

Dr. Seuss, sitting in his office which is on top of an old watchtower.

Dr. Seuss's Horton Hears a Who *was written after he visited Hiroshima, Japan. It was a city destroyed in WWII.*

THE LORAX

Perhaps the most famous Dr. Seuss book with a message is *The Lorax*. It is about a greedy Once-ler and his family who move into a forest of Truffula Trees. The Once-lers want to cut down all the Truffula Trees to make hairy pink underwear called Thneeds.

Another small creature called the Lorax lives in the forest. He asks the Once-lers not to cut down all the trees, but they won't listen. As the Once-lers cut down more and more Truffula Trees, the skies over the forest become polluted. The water becomes filled with Gluppity-Glup. The Lorax loses its home.

Some people were angry when they heard the Lorax story. One town in California tried to ban the book from the local library. Many of the people who lived in the town were in the logging business. They thought *The Lorax* taught children that trees should not be cut down.

Geisel defended his book. He said it "is about people who harm the environment and leave nothing behind."

He said he wanted to use it to teach children to pre-serve the environment. Or, as the Lorax says in the book, "Plant a new Truffula. Treat it with care. Give it clean water. And feed it fresh air."

THE WORK OF WRITING

The Lorax is the only book Geisel wrote which people have tried to ban. It also is his favorite book and took the least time of any to write.

"We were at an inn in Kenya (Africa), and I was sitting near a swimming pool," Geisel said. "About a mile away, a herd of elephants came over a hill. I don't know what happened. I grabbed a laundry list that I had beside me and wrote the whole book in 45 minutes."

Most of the time, Geisel said writing a book is not so easy. "When I start a new book, I'll noodle things over and develop some characters," he said. "Most of them go in the wastebasket, but a couple get in conflict. Then words begin to come. If I get stuck mentally in a story, I'll draw my way out. Other times, I write the whole thing without any illustrations."

"If I start with a two-headed animal, I must never waver from that concept," he added. "There must be two hats in the closet, two toothbrushes in the bathroom and two sets of spectacles on the night table."

Geisel is different from many writers in that all of his books are in rhyme. Geisel said writing those rhymes can be difficult. He once compared writing rhymes to unraveling a sock. If the final line of the rhyme doesn't work, "You take some of your best stuff and throw it away," he said.

To form his rhymes, Geisel often made up new words. When he wrote *Yertle the Turtle*, he had to get special permission from his publisher to use an existing word. "I used the word burp, and nobody had ever burped before on the pages of a children's book," Geisel said. "It took a decision from the president of the publishing house before my vulgar turtle was permitted to do so."

Theodore Seuss Geisel, one of the most celebrated authors of children's books.

25

THE WORLD'S FAVORITE DOCTOR

Geisel's unique cartoons and writing style have earned him worldwide recognition. He received a Pulitzer citation, which is one of the highest honors a writer can achieve. He also won an Emmy Award for the animated television show *How the Grinch Stole Christmas*.

Nationally, an exhibit of Geisel's work toured the U.S. for three years. The National Association of Elementary School Principals honored him for his work as well. When Geisel would visit elementary schools, he often was greeted by children dressed up as the Cat in the Hat. Even Dartmouth College, where he went to school, granted him an honorary doctorate degree.

Geisel's popularity was especially clear on his birthday. He would receive up to 20,000 birthday cards a year. Geisel said the local post office grew to dread March 2. "The post office is not delighted with the packages that ooze broken green eggs or uncapped bottles of gooey Oobleck," he said.

*Dr. Seuss's 44 childrens books have been translated into 20
languages and sold more than 100 million copies worldwide.*

Most of Geisel's fans are children, even though he and Helen never had children of their own. Geisel said people often asked him if he liked children. He would reply, "I like children in the same way that I like people. There are some stinkers among children as well as adults. I like or dislike them as individuals."

Geisel also received many invitations to speak. Once, a college near Chicago asked him to give the address on graduation day. Geisel's speech was a poem he had written. It was called "My Uncle Terwilliger on the Art of Eating Popovers." The poem took him exactly one minute and 14 seconds to recite:

My uncle ordered popovers from the restaurant's bill of fare.
And, when they were served, he regarded them with a penetrating stare...
Then he spoke great Words of Wisdom as he sat there on the chair:
"To eat these things," said my uncle,
"You must exercise great care.
You may swallow down what's solid...
BUT ... you must spit out the air!"

And...as you partake of the world's bill of fare,
That's darned good advice to follow.
Do a lot of spitting out the hot air.
And be careful what you swallow.

A BOOK FOR GRANDPARENTS

In 1986, Geisel took a break from doing children's stories to write a book for adults. The book, *You're Only Old Once!*, was about the trials of seeing doctors. Now more than 80 years old, Geisel felt he was spending too much time in doctors' waiting rooms.

"The waits were most unpleasant," he said. "I began to take my sketch pads with me and amused myself by thinking of the horrible things they were going to do to me next. Gradually words came too."

You're Only Old Once! sold more than a million copies in the first year alone. It also rose to the top of the combined fiction/nonfiction best-seller list.

Bob Keeshan, "Captain Kangaroo" was a good friend of Dr. Seuss.

A LEGACY OF LAUGHTER

Geisel died on September 24, 1991, at his home in California. His first wife, Helen, had died 24 years earlier. Geisel's second wife, Audrey, continues to live in their hilltop home.

Geisel's death was met with many tears and fond memories. Peter Bernstein, whose father was Dr. Seuss's publisher, recalled, "Any Seuss fan knows he loved to make up silly names and use them to good effect. When he needed a plumber, he would call and say that the dipilator was broken. The plumber, embarrassed to admit his ignorance of dipilators, would show up promptly."

Another friend of Geisel's was Bob Keeshan, television's Captain Kangaroo. "He tried to emphasize strong values that not only children but adults need to have in this world," Keeshan said.

The world will miss Dr. Seuss. Fortunately, all the Sneeches and Zooks and Once-lers are as close as the nearest library. And they'll be there for a long, long time.

The world will miss Dr. Seuss.